"An awesome contribution…"

—William F. Buckley, Jr., concert harpsichordist, musicologist, inventor of the Buckley musical notation system, author, publisher of *The National Review,* and moderator (retired) of the television show "Firing Line."

"An excellent solution…"

—Reginald Gerig, Chairman Emeritus of the Piano Department, Wheaton Conservatory of Music.

HOW TO MAKE YOUR PIANO

SING LIKE A VIOLIN

How to Make Your Piano Sing Like a Violin

Perfecting Your Touch at the Piano

Larry Greenfield

Unlimited Publishing

Bloomington, Indiana

Distributing Publisher:
Unlimited Publishing, LLC
Bloomington, Indiana
http://www.unlimitedpublishing.com

Cover and Book Design by Charles King

This book was typeset with Adobe® InDesign™, with headings in the Adobe® Jensen™ Multiple Master typeface and text in the Adobe Garamond® typeface.

ISBN 1-58832-018-9

Unlimited Publishing

Bloomington, Indiana

The impetus for creativity comes not from having a new idea, but from an obsession with the idea that what has been said is not enough.

—Eugene Delacroix

Table of Contents

Introduction

THIS BOOK IS ABOUT one vital pianistic skill: *touch.* Touch creates gradations of sound. It is the pathway through which the player expresses emotions. I have discovered a method by which the touch can be independently, directly, and dramatically improved, thereby vastly improving the sounds that you produce from the piano. It is applicable to all styles, to all levels of ability, and to all levels of commitment. The book and the method are directed primarily, but not solely, toward the serious pianist.

However, not everyone has the talent or the desire to get to Carnegie Hall, Birdland, Nashville, whatever. There is good news for the more casual pianists, which probably includes the vast majority of children taking piano lessons, in addition to an array of non-playing adults who took lessons as kids. My method is very easy to do and, after a minute's warm-up, you can actually go directly to practicing pieces. That's because this method, while primarily developed to give you a fine touch, secondarily will also give you all the finger articulation you will need. So, happily, all those exercises you have probably found so tedious and boring will be rendered superfluous. And practicing with my method will actually give you melodic rewards as you proceed. In other words, your natural desire to play better with the least amount of extra effort will be fulfilled.

But, whether you're committed or casual, you'll find the immediate change in your piano playing exciting. That I guarantee.

Dedication

To my wife Elaine,
my son Devon,
and my uncle Jack.

Special Thanks

Special thanks to my artist, Helmut Eppich; to Len Kusnetz, Laura Hodes, Bradley Kantor, Sandra Sider, and Devon Greenfield for their invaluable suggestions; to Elaine Greenfield, editor extraordinary; to Vladimir Horowitz, whose hand position piqued my curiosity and prompted a voyage of discovery; and to John T. Dugan, whose "Columbo" script gave me a 'Eureka' moment.

Prologue

VLADIMIR HOROWITZ came out of one of his retirements in 1967 and played a concert at Carnegie Hall. The TV close-ups amazed me. He played with his fingers comparatively flat upon the keys. After all, the virtually universal approach to playing and teaching the piano was with rounded fingers. I asked myself why the pianist who was hailed as head and shoulders above the rest of us didn't play the keys like the rest of us.

Years later I learned from research that Rachmaninoff, the 'elder statesman,' had befriended the young Horowitz early in the 20th century. He said that Horowitz played all wrong but that his technique worked for him. In other words, Rachmaninoff felt that Horowitz's hand position was idiosyncratic to Horowitz, not for general use.

At the time, without academic background, I said to myself that if Horowitz played better with flat fingers than anyone else playing with rounded fingers, then he must know something that we don't know. Actually, I never did find out the basis of his technique. However, watching Horowitz so excited me that I decided to develop a practicing method with flat fingers to improve my touch. Little did I know what I'd started. Fifteen years later I had created my own method for practicing with flat fingers. And then, on one of those days when mortality looks back at you in the mirror, I realized that if I kept it to myself, the knowledge would die with me. If at all possible, I didn't want that to happen.

However, that meant writing a book, something that was not my forte. But I didn't see that I had any other choice. Another eighteen years went into that project. There were countless hours of library research, lessons and books on anatomy (which gave me new respect for anyone who gets through the first year of medical school), and rewriting ad nauseam. When I finally finished the book I felt great satisfaction that I had created something I thought was worth doing but at the same time, great relief that the work was finally over.

Now came the pragmatic part of getting it into other people's hands. I found that publishers and agents were not interested in a book on piano technique. Oh, they all thought the content was terrific. It was just a little thing like marketing. They didn't think, given the American public's taste for law, sex, and violence, that a book on piano technique would give them sufficient return to justify spending the money to publish it. I had to admit I could see their point. So I paid to publish it, still determined to give my method to others so that you, dear reader, can play the piano more beautifully than you ever thought you could. If you're reading this, thanks for letting this idea live.

Chapter 1

Two Schools of Thought

MANY PIANO STUDENTS are taught to begin practicing with scales and the exercises of Hanon, Czerny, et al. Generally, the student may be given very little theoretical justification for these procedures. The student may be merely told that this is the time-honored way in which practicing must be done. Students may be told that the purpose of these exercises is to strengthen the fingers equally. Many people seem to have accepted without question the 'traditional' way to practice and have very strong opinions in its favor.

As a matter of fact, though, several theorists have argued against the practicing of scales and the exercises of Hanon, Czerny, etc. on several grounds. One criticism that has been put forth is that the training, which these exercises provide, is not transferable to playing pieces, but rather constitutes training only for playing the exercises themselves. Whiteside, for instance, was completely against the traditional exercise regimen, and held that practicing Chopin's Etudes would give the pianist all the necessary training for playing anything.

Another criticism of traditional training has been that its aim of achieving equal strength in all the fingers is doomed to failure. Anatomically, some fingers are stronger than others. Equality of finger strength will simply never be possible. In fact, in terms of the thumb, as you will see, such an aim is counterproductive. Some theorists have said that it is not necessary to try to achieve that equality in order to achieve power in one's playing. They argue that the proper use of forearm rotation and wrist undulation will maximize the capability of each finger. Therefore, it is entirely possible that the traditional canon of exercises is superfluous, to say nothing of being tedious and boring.

However, the point is that all the viewpoints and traditional techniques only train one set of muscles. That is not enough. As you will see, there are other muscles which are vital to achieving a fine touch. Up until now, those muscles have been overlooked.

There are two dimensions to the physical playing of keys on a piano: the vertical and the horizontal. The vertical dimension concerns the production of individual notes. Obviously, a downward action is needed to depress a key and produce a tone, and a corresponding upward action is needed to release that key and cease the production of that tone (of course it is physically possible to hold down a key indefinitely until the vibrations of the strings, and therefore the tone, have stopped, but since that concept is not useful for general purposes we will disregard it).

The horizontal dimension is the consecutive production of notes which constitute the melody, harmony, rhythm, etc. How these dimensions are fused results in, as the case may be, beautiful or not beautiful piano playing.

In general, two schools of pianistic thought have arisen—the artistic (e.g. Deppe, Leimer and Gieseking, Newman, Lhevine, Whiteside), and the scientific (e.g. Ortmann, Matthay, Schultz, Fielden). It would be unfair and inaccurate to state that the artistic side was concerned with the horizontal dimension of playing and the scientific side with the vertical dimension, although some emphasis in those directions was apparent from research. In fact, some of the 'artistic' theorists discussed bones, muscles, and nerves, and some of the 'scientific' theorists discussed phrases, etc. Nevertheless, perhaps due to nothing more than antithetical temperament, there does not seem to have been general acceptance of each other's point of view, although so much seemed admirable and applicable from both camps.

Chapter 2

What's Been Missing

There is one thing the two schools of thought seem to have in common. When discussing the vertical dimension, the production of a single tone, everyone seems to have made a major logical error. The production of a single tone can be divided into three major phases: one, the preparation for making the tone; two, the actual playing of the key; and three, the release of the key and the cessation of the note. Almost every theorist emphasized the first two phases, each according to individual theoretical inclinations.

By the same token, almost everyone spent very, very little time and energy on phase three. One 'merely' releases the muscles that have played the note, or if one's technique is 'proper' the release will become part of the flow. Some books, two hundred pages long, spend a few sentences, a paragraph, or at most half a page on phase three. It was viewed as 'obvious' that the fingers simply get off the keys. The process of getting off the keys was not even considered worth thinking about, much less something to be practiced. The only writer who even suggested that the finger must also be conscious of the way in which it lets the depressed key rise again was Marie Jaell, teacher of Albert Schweitzer, who had learned it from her teacher, Franz Liszt.

Giving short shrift to phase three (getting off the keys) is not logical. Perhaps the importance of getting off the keys would be better appreciated if we look for analogies. In sports in which an instrument is wielded against a ball (e.g. golf, baseball, tennis) it is widely recognized that the follow-through is an integral part of the swing, indeed that a poor follow-through is itself indicative of an incorrect swing. In baseball there is a controversy between the Charley Lau school of thought that the top hand should be removed from the bat on the follow-through, and the Ted Williams contention that the top hand is the power hand and that its removal on the follow-through is a mistake. No matter what one's opinion is, no one seriously concerned with baseball considers this controversy pointless. This is so because the follow-through is a crucial part of the swing and the physical results are immediately palpable. Without going through a parallel analysis in golf and tennis, follow-through is vital to technique in those sports as well.

Matters are different with the piano. The effects of the follow-through (getting off the keys) are not so obvious. Yet it is crucial to a good touch. Regardless of how or from what direction one strikes a particular key, its corresponding note will resound. The note will be correct, but it may or may not sound good to the ear. Rapid articulation of the keys and firm fortes can mask tonal problems. Taking the follow-through for granted has been occurring since Christofori invented the pianoforte in 1709. It is my thesis that this oversight is incorrect and that a trained follow-through is necessary to create a really fine touch.

Perhaps two other sports analogies will make this clearer. A weight-lifter, when pressing a hand weight, pulls the weight close to his shoulder, bringing the upper arm parallel to the torso, thus contracting his biceps muscles and expanding his triceps muscles (on the underside of his arm). When he extends the weight so that his entire arm is straight and perpendicular to his torso, the opposite occurs: his triceps muscles are contracted and his biceps muscles are expanded. If you have ever observed this done, you may have noticed how slowly the extension can be made and retracted, with consummate control over the route both ways. This control derives from the balance of the biceps and triceps muscles.

Recent developments in sports science are perhaps even more revealing. Someone has noted, in comparing athletes from various major team sports, that baseball players have had a statistically significantly greater amount of hamstring pulls than basketball players. After study, the conclusion was reached that the reason for this is that basketball players are required to move backwards when playing defense, something which is not required of baseball players as a general rule. Running backwards contracts the hamstrings; running forward extends the hamstrings while simultaneously contracting the quadriceps (the front thigh muscles). Apparently, the more balanced development of hamstring and quadriceps muscles in basketball players lessens the frequency of hamstring pulls.

Certainly Major League baseball players have a vested interest in keeping their bodies in top condition. Yet many still suffer hamstring injuries. Their conditioning programs are evidently overlooking something. It is not that their programs are incorrect; it is that the programs may be conceptually incomplete. Some trainers seem to have instituted programs which include running backward in the sand. This may indicate that there is an increasing awareness of the importance of muscle balance.

In "The Game According To Syd," Syd Thrift pointed out that a baseball player usually works the agnostic muscles: quadriceps, pectorals, etc., but ignores the antagonistic muscles: hamstrings and muscles in the back of the shoulder. Thrift reported that a conditioning consultant for the Giants and Yankees had begun to utilize specific exercises for the antagonistic muscles of the legs and arms in order to maintain muscle balance in the limbs, thus improving conditioning and reducing the incidence of hamstring pulls.

Muscle imbalance as a cause of injuries isn't just important in athletics. When I did my research, I was quite surprised to discover that the number of injuries, for example tendonitis and stress, that pianists incur is considerably higher than one would ordinarily suppose from chance. In fact, I learned of a doctor who specializes only in musician's injuries, especially pianist's. This research increased my conviction that I was on the right track. I was more than ever convinced that existing piano theories were flawed. Not that they were incorrect. But that they were incomplete. Something was missing.

A dramatic example of conceptual incompleteness can be seen in a far different field: the early growth of Psychoanalysis. Freud wrote that in the beginning years of his practice, he gave many dream interpretations which he was convinced were accurate. Yet he was often met with vehement denials from his patients. At first this puzzled him. But as treatments progressed, he came to realize that his prior interpretations had not been incorrect, only incomplete. The patient's vehement denials had really been directed at what he had not said. When the omitted material eventually came to light, those missing pieces validated his earlier interpretations.

As in the above examples of baseball and psychoanalysis, piano technique has also been plagued with conceptual incompleteness. In order to find that something which is missing in existing piano techniques, we will begin with physical realities and build from that foundation. Playing a note means depressing a key from its normal resting state, through its let-off (the point at which the hammer is tripped), down to the key bed (the bottom of the keyboard), and then releasing the key.

The changes in the volume of the notes are controlled by the speed with which the hammers strike the strings. According to Ortmann, the power used should be sufficient so that the hammer travels the last eighth of an inch to the strings within a range of hundred-thousandths of a second. At 416 hundred-thousandths of a second, the softest sound discernible by the human ear will be produced; at 51 hundred-thousandths of a second, the loudest sound will be produced.

Godowsky made the useful distinction between technique and mechanics. Technique embraces all facets of playing, including feelings. Mechanics are the actual bodily movements involved in playing. I am writing about mechanics. Proper training in mechanics is the essential precursor to proper muscle balance and, therefore, to a complete technique.

My method will give you control over how much pressure you want to use to depress each key. To obtain delicate control of the piano keys the pianist must understand how to bring the muscles into balance, like the weight lifter, the basketball player, and the baseball player who trains running backwards in the sand. Proper balance will create a state of alert readiness in the muscles, with a controlled sensitivity capable of producing a beautiful, singing tone. It is to the mechanics of how to achieve that state of responsiveness that we now turn.

Chapter 3

The Remedy: Exercises for Fingers 2, 3, 4 & 5

All skeletal muscles fall into two categories: flexors and extensors, which act just as their names suggest. Skeletal muscles are reciprocal; that is, they work together in pairs. Flexors reciprocate extensors, and vice-versa. For example, the quadriceps and the hamstrings are reciprocal muscles of the femur (thighbone). Each kind of muscle accomplishes its function by the process of contraction. To cease their action the muscles expand, reverting to either a resting state or a state of readiness. As mentioned above, it is when these reciprocal muscles are in balance that we see a well-controlled action. Let us now look at how this applies to the piano.

Depressing a key on the piano predominantly involves the contraction of the flexor muscles in the forearm. However, the release of the key involves not just the extension of the previously contracted flexor muscles. Raising the finger off the key also involves the contraction of the reciprocal extensor muscles in the forearm. These muscles are relatively so small that this is not readily palpable. But it happens.

This simple fact, that reciprocal forearm muscle action is involved in getting off a key, has far-reaching implications. It appears that all known techniques and methods of instruction, directly or by implication, deal only with the contraction of the flexors. They all seem to ignore the fact that the extensor muscles contract as the key is released. Therefore, except for physical geniuses, the reciprocal muscles of most pianists' hands are not harmoniously developed, and thus are not balanced. The flexors are dominating the extensors. As a result, the overwhelming majority of piano tones are too harsh. The original name 'pianoforte' sounds too often as if it should have been shortened to 'forte' instead of to 'piano.' When was the last time you heard someone play the piano and you thought they were playing too softly? The factor of muscle imbalance must be recognized and addressed as a significant component in developing a delicate touch, if a training program is to be really complete.

Moreover, my new methodology will demonstrate this connection to be not some vague, abstract theory. Instead I'm presenting something which anyone and everyone can immediately apply and feel directly in their hands within a few minutes of practicing. That something will change your touch, your tone, and your method of practicing forever.

I have created training exercises to establish muscle balance in the hands and forearms by strengthening the previously neglected extensor muscles. For each note practiced, for each flexor (agonistic muscle) contraction, I have created a corresponding extensor (antagonistic muscle) contraction. I want to emphasize that this training is to be done during practice time only; its effects will then be felt during actual playing.

This chapter will describe how the training is done with the second, third, fourth, and fifth fingers. However, the thumb moves in an oppositional direction to the other four fingers. This difference is so significant that it requires a variation of its own, which will be dealt with in the next chapter.

It is imperative to begin the training one finger at a time. Once this is accomplished, there will be adjustments for intervals and chords. The concept is to contract only the muscles to be trained. Those muscles and their 'neighbors' must be relaxed prior to exercising them, lest tension interfere with and negate the effect of the exercises. The fingers may be exercised in any order, as long as no fingers are omitted.

In order to isolate and exercise the extensor muscles fully, I found that I needed to have an external resistance for them to act upon. The sides of the black keys serve this purpose admirably. During the training exercise practice on the white keys only. Omit those white keys which do not have a black key adjacent in the direction of middle C. In other words, omit C and F for the right hand, E and B for the left hand.

Step I

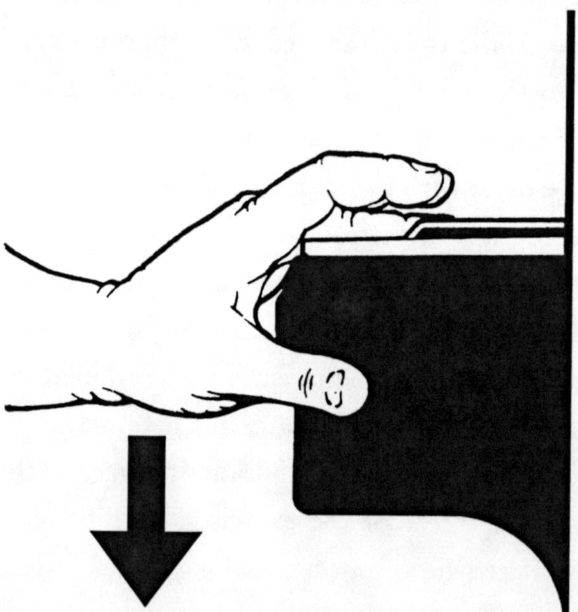

Step I

Let us begin with the third finger of the left hand. Place the top of the left palm against the frame of the piano, with the third finger resting flat, just above and approximately parallel to the A key just below middle C.

The wrist will be in low position. The second, fourth, and fifth fingers will also be flat above the keys next to the A key.

Hold this position for a count of one second. Just saying the word 'and,' either to yourself or aloud, is a good way to do that.

Step II

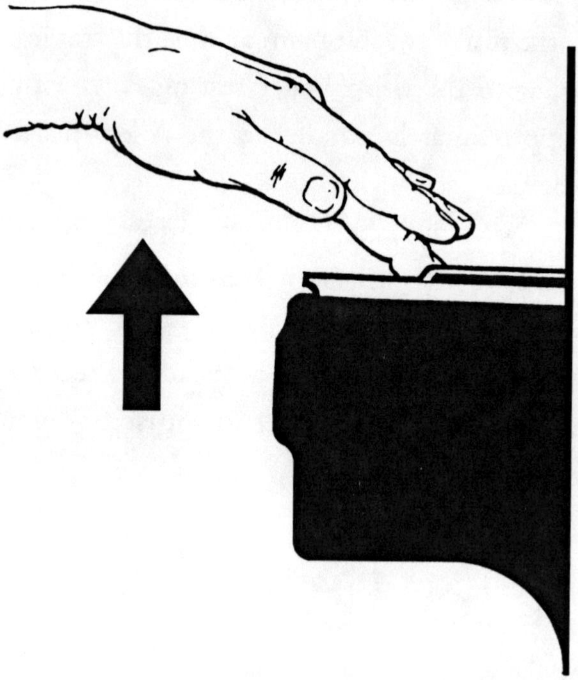

Step II

Raise the left wrist into moderately high position, above the keyboard, until the finger is at an angle of about 30 to 45 degrees to the key. As you raise the wrist, the third finger will gradually depress the A key. Maintain the finger contact with the key on the flat, palm side of the last finger segment, the side opposite the fingernail, as opposed to the tip of the finger. The finger segments, divided by knuckles, are called phalanxes; the first phalanx is the one nearest the hand; the last phalanx holds the fingernail. Hold that position and say the word 'and.'

This gradual depression will prevent tension forming in the hand and fingers. It will also promote more control, and therefore a better touch, than merely hitting the key like a loose hammer with little control over how much force to use. However, as you will see, the real key to a finer touch lies further on.

Maintaining contact on the key with the palm side of the last phalanx instead of the tip will promote a finer touch. Keeping pressure away from the very tip of the finger will also help prevent the possibility of any injury—no small consideration.

Step III

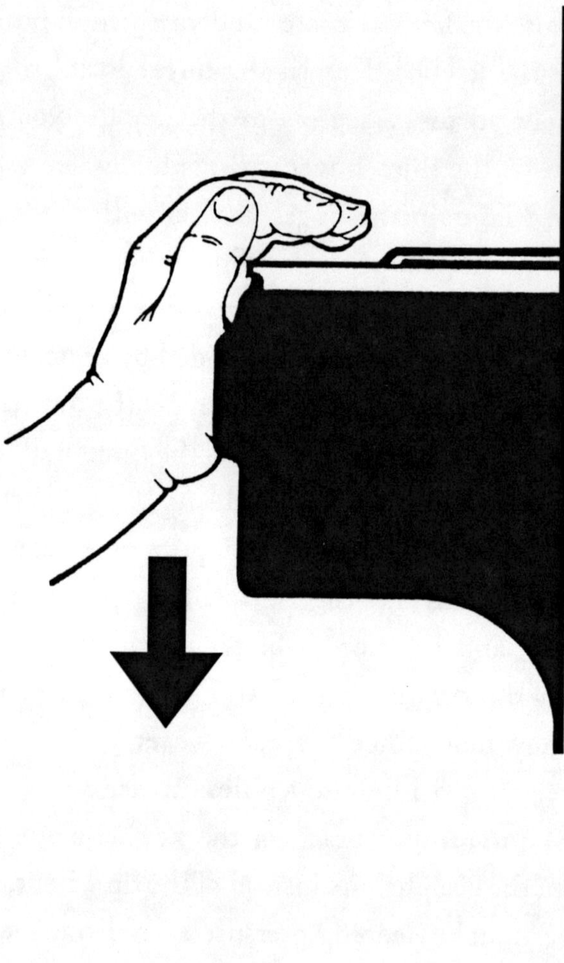

Step III

Step III is the point of departure from all known techniques of the past. At this juncture pianists normally merely lift their finger off the key and then practice the next key, thereby inadvertently neglecting the development of their forearm extensor muscles. That omission, as you will see, obviates the conditions which would create a beautiful, singing tone.

You are about to learn to do the reverse: to learn how to practice a follow-through that harmonizes and balances muscle development, thereby establishing the proper conditions for producing singing piano tones.

It is at this point, Step III, that the key to a really fine touch begins. There are two exercises, Steps III and IV, both of which exercise the forearm extensor muscles. Step III flows right into Step IV and practicing them both together as one, will maximize their effects. Later on, when we get to the actual practicing of pieces, situational adjustments will be discussed.

Gradually lower the left wrist into low position, this time with the entire palm touching the piano frame. Relax the hand completely when you contact the piano frame. In the process, the third finger may or may not rise off the key. Hold that position and say the word 'and.' For convenience I will refer to Step III as the 'drop' movement.

This movement, in the opposite direction that the fingers and hands ordinarily move when playing or practicing the piano, contracts the extensor muscles in the forearm, although not to the maximum degree possible and desirable. For that we must include Step IV.

Technically, we have combined what is called, in anatomical jargon, an eccentric exercise (Step III) with a concentric exercise (Step II). When a muscle is activated the muscles and tendons, again in anatomical jargon, 'fire.' The mechanical efficiency of eccentric exercises, although not constant, is generally substantially higher than that of concentric exercises. The combination of both eccentric and concentric exercises causes an effect called the restitution of elastic energy, and forms the natural type of muscle function known as the stretch-shortening cycle. That restitution of elastic energy allows the concentric action to take place with greater power than can be initiated by concentric exercise alone.

For the second, third, fourth, and fifth fingers, the force developed by extrinsic muscles is far greater than the force developed by intrinsic muscles. But it is important to note that for the thumbs this development is reversed! For the thumbs, the force developed by the intrinsic muscles is far greater than the force developed by the extrinsic muscles. This fact reinforces the need for a separate exercise for the thumbs. This will be dealt with in the next chapter.

Step IVa

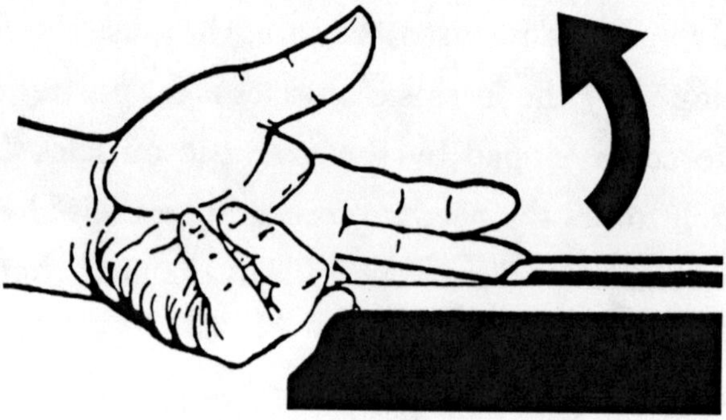

Step IVb

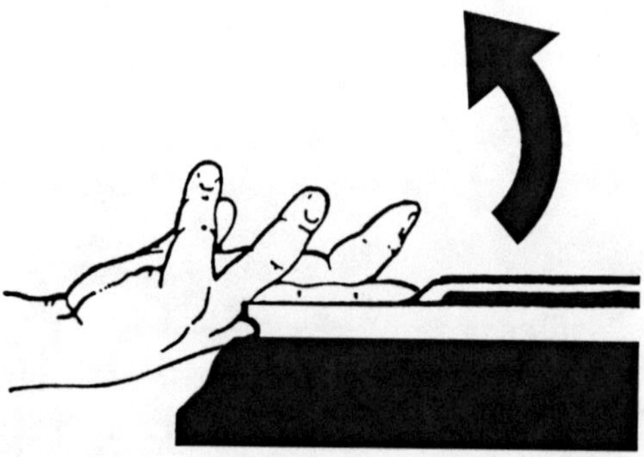

Step IV

This Step is the key idea in practicing for a fine touch. The previous Step III, in addition to contracting the forearm extensor muscles, also performed the vital function of being an indispensable precursor to launching the movement of Step IV.

Slowly lift the left hand (depressing the A key again if you raised it off the key in Step III), slide the last phalanx of the third finger forward and, as you do so, rotate the adjacent finger nearest the thumb, in this case the index (second) finger, counterclockwise 180 degrees. This will cause the third finger and indeed the entire left hand to rotate counterclockwise. In other words, the finger being exercised is depressing the key. Rotating the adjacent finger does the work of pulling the hand up and over. This action allows the finger being exercised to remain passive, with a minimum of muscle resistance and a maximum of extensor muscle receptivity. As you do so, exert pressure with the third finger against the adjacent black key to your right and lower your wrist to the level of the keyboard. The wrist and hand will now be in a supinated (face up) position. The inverted third finger will now rest upon the depressed A key. Hold this position and say the word 'and.'

This critical rotation constitutes the smallest, discrete, 'practice-able' unit in piano practice. This exercise, except for the thumbs, is how to practice getting off the keys! It demonstrates how to convert the silent space/time between two notes into a meaningful component of a delicate touch. By practicing Steps I through V the finger will acquire much more power and control, leading to a much finer touch than if the finger were merely exercised by playing down on the key and then releasing it in the conventional manner.

This principle of indirect exercise is a basic tenet here and will hold for all the fingers, including the thumb, as you will see. After you finish the thumb section you will be able to easily verify all that I say, simply by doing these exercises yourself.

Step V

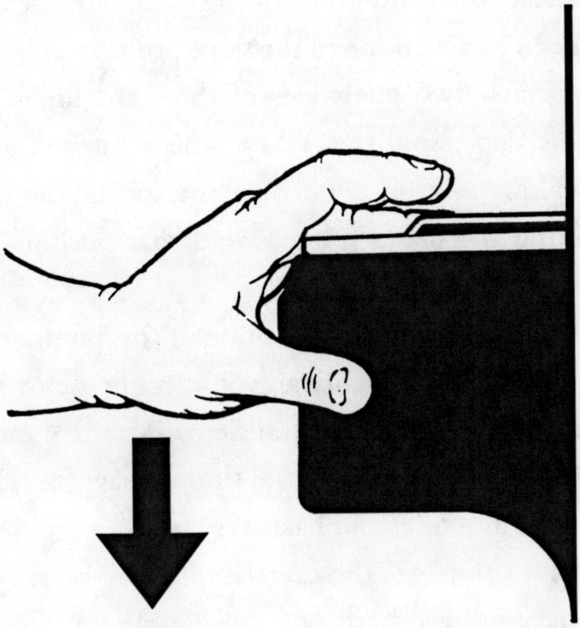

Step V

Rotate the third finger of the left hand clockwise 180 degrees, returning to the same position as in Step I. The first two phalanxes of the third finger will resume depressing the A key. The wrist will again be in low position, with only the top of the palm touching the piano frame. Hold that position and say the word 'and.'

There is an additional option at this point. Since Steps I and V are identical, you can choose to keep the key depressed and repeat Steps IV and V on the same key once more or several times. I have found the resulting muscular emphasis very useful.

That completes the exercises for one finger. You will have utilized both types of muscle contractions, concentric and eccentric, and possibly a third type, isometric, and you will have exercised the extensor muscles and, in Step II, to some degree the flexor muscles as well. Your anatomy will now be ready to practice the next note.

Step VI

Repeat the exercises described above for the second, fourth, and fifth fingers individually. For the second finger, rotate the thumb counter-clockwise; for the fourth finger rotate the third finger counter-clockwise; for the fifth finger rotate the fourth finger counter-clockwise. Use the two octaves below middle C.

Upon the start of the rotation, retract the fingers not being exercised, which are farthest from the thumb, at the middle knuckle and duck them under whatever finger is resting on the key. This will happen naturally. It simply necessitates raising the first two finger phalanxes of the finger being exercised high enough for the other fingers to pass under them.

Remember to use only keys which have an adjacent black key to the right. In other words, omit Bs and Es in practicing the left hand. Repeat this exercise only until you feel that each finger is sufficiently warmed up, which, of course, will be a subjective judgment on your part.

Step VII

When the left-hand warm-up is completed, repeat Steps I to VI for the right hand. When you change to the right hand use the two octaves above middle C. Use only those keys which have an adjacent black key to the left. In other words, Cs and Fs will be omitted. The direction of the rotation in steps IV and V will now be reversed. That is, the right hand will perform the rotation in a clockwise direction from Step III to Step IV. Then, at the end of Step IV, the right hand will pronate (turn the palm down) in a counter-clockwise direction and retract until the right palm is again partly against the frame of the piano just as it was in Step III. Again, do these exercises only until you feel that the right hand is sufficiently warmed up.

Incidentally, my method seems to have solved the problem which so plagued Robert Schumann. The ligaments on either side of the fourth finger connect its tendon to the tendons of the third and fifth fingers. That limits the extension (but not the flexion) of the fourth finger, impeding its independent functioning to a significant degree.

Schumann tried a mechanical device that was intended to substantially increase the fourth finger's independence. One source claimed that he even underwent an operation to try to achieve freedom for his fourth finger. All in vain. Tragically, Schumann's finger was injured permanently and evidently he never played again. Imagine how such a dreadful outcome must have exacerbated his already severe mental problems.

Schumann knew that something was needed to overcome the impediment to the fourth finger. Sadly, he just didn't know how to get there. According to Ortmann, "no amount of practice can overcome entirely this physiological limitation." Up until now, no one has seriously challenged that point of view. But now, with my practicing program, indeed you can do what eluded Schumann. You can overcome that fourth finger impediment, to the point where you can achieve a tone with the fourth finger which will astonish you.

Chapter 4

The Remedy: Exercises for the Thumbs

We now turn to the all-important thumbs. Bach seems to have been the first to emphasize them, but down through the years many piano theorists, among them Paderewski, have accentuated them. So their emphasis certainly has an illustrious musical parentage.

Think of the many things you did this morning with your hands: washing, dressing, combing your hair, eating, perhaps making a phone call, etc.—all made possible by the miraculous action of the thumbs in opposition to the other four fingers. That opposition is their natural mode of functioning, and is one of the distinguishing physical characteristics of human beings. Just think of lions, horses, etc., animals possessing much greater strength and speed than we, but unable to even approach our dexterity due to their lack of opposable thumbs.

Playing the piano is one of the very few human activities where the thumb is required to do something unnatural, namely act in concert (no pun intended) with the other four fingers. This physical reality creates serious problems for the thumb and its musculature and, ultimately, for the pianist's touch.

Compare the piano to the typewriter or computer, where the thumbs are used in their natural oppositional mode, only for the space bar, not for typing the keys. Other musical instruments, violin, clarinet, timpani, utilize the thumbs in their natural oppositional mode as well. But on the piano, our opposable thumbs are forced to function in the same direction as the other fingers. This is completely antithetical to their structure.

Clearly, exercises for the thumb had to be somewhat different from the exercises for the other four fingers, if only because of the difference in anatomical placement. The thumb movement begins at the wrist joint; the movement of the other fingers begins at the distal end of the palm of the hand.

The drop (Step III, above) worked to some degree for the thumb, at least as far as the forearm extensor muscles were concerned. But the drop did not address the musculature between the thumb and the other fingers. First of all there remained too much tension there, and second of all the extensors there remained unexercised and therefore imbalanced—still an impediment to a fine touch.

For a long time I struggled with rotations for the thumbs like those for the other fingers, albeit with considerable variations of detail. Each time I thought I finally 'had it,' but in the end each new variation only worked partially, remaining elusively incomplete.

And then it hit me—I had it reversed! To exercise the muscles around the thumb I had to leave the thumb immobile (!) after a key was depressed. To exercise the more powerful intrinsic thumb muscles, the thenars, I had to move the index finger!

Of course no muscle functions totally in isolation—the 'simplest' movements require the coordination of several muscles. But for the sake of simplicity I have referred to the main muscles involved and assumed the cooperation of its neighbors. There are external and internal thenar muscles in the hand which, in addition to the structure of the thumb, play a big role in allowing the greater flexibility of the thumb than the other fingers.

The internal thenar muscles are located in the fleshy part of the hand between the thumb and index finger. The external thenar muscles are located in the fleshy part of the hand at the base of the thumb.

Ordinarily, when one depresses a key with the thumb, the external thenars are contracted. When one raises the finger off the key, the external thenars are released and extended; simultaneously the internal thenars are contracted, but so slightly as to be hardly palpable. This creates a hidden problem—a thumb whose muscles are out of balance. Just imagine how hard the thumb will then hit a key, resulting in too harsh a tone.

However, when the index finger is flexed the internal thenars are contracted. This contraction is easily palpable and visible, as that fleshy part tenses and bulges out. The internal thenars control adduction (movement toward the hand) of the thumb, the kind of movement necessary for the removal of the thumb from a key after the key has been played. These muscles tire easily. Therefore, exercising the internal thenar muscles will build both balance and endurance for the thumbs, thereby improving their touch. (As an unanticipated bonus, I also found my thumb articulation vastly improved.)

When one employs the ensuing thumb exercises, the thumb and the other four fingers will actually work as two separate but related parts of a single entity. Their automatic synchronization will give you control over how much power you use when you strike a key. Without these thumb exercises too much tension remains in parts of the hands, too much unrestricted, uncontrolled energy is poured into the keys. This is why you may have heard many people play the piano too loudly, but in all probability have never heard anyone play the piano too softly.

My primary anatomical consultant, Dr. John Palo, informed me of two relevant facts. First, thumb movements are extremely complicated. They have been the objects of many analyses by medical professionals, who have frequently disagreed with each other. The complexity is such that sometimes when an author presented an original idea, he or she often created his or her own terminology. This complicated the field all the more.

Secondly, Dr. Palo informed me that my thumb exercise constituted a pioneering effort not only in music, but perhaps even in anatomy! In this diverse area there really isn't any definitive anatomical corroboration. So for corroboration I will rely solely on you, dear reader. If you venture to employ my exercises, the proof will be in your pudding, as it has been in mine.

Thumb Step I

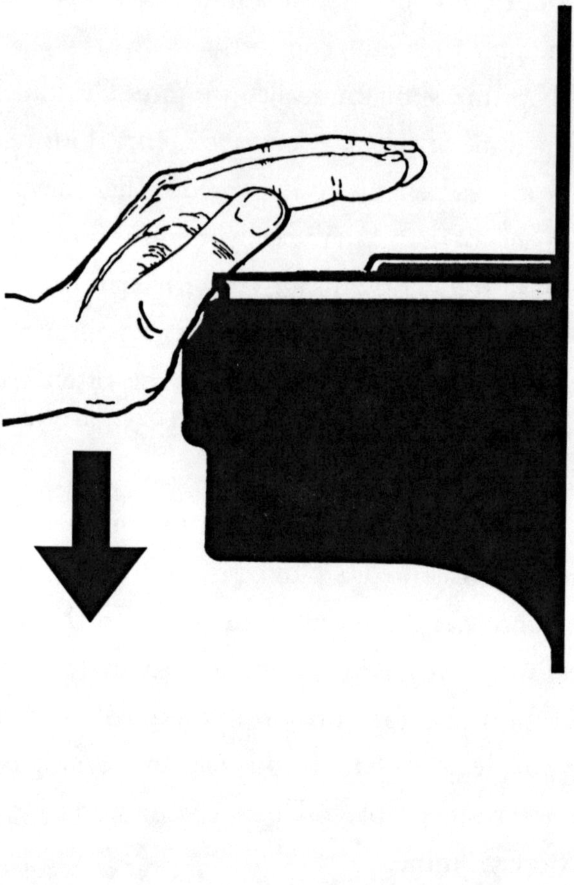

Thumb Step I

Place the top of the left palm against the piano frame at about a 45 degree angle to the keyboard. Rest the first phalanx (nearest the hand) of the left thumb against the edge of any white key in the two octaves below middle C. The wrist will be in low position. Hold that position and say the word 'and.'

Thumb Step II

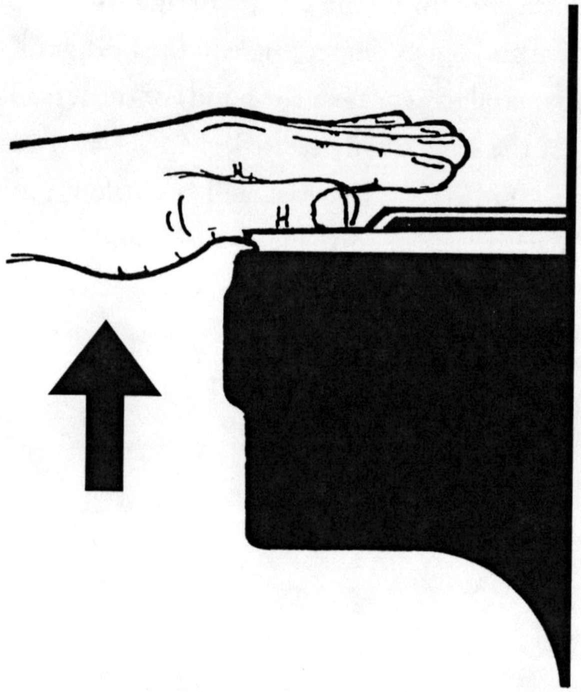

Thumb Step II

Move the wrist up, thus depressing the key with last phalanx and part of the first phalanx of the thumb, causing the note to play. Hold that position and say the word 'and.'

The second or index finger will naturally be positioned close to the thumb. Mine is one and a half to two keys away. Yours may be closer or farther away from your thumb, depending upon the physical construction of your hand. Regardless of the spread between your thumb and index finger, the point is to obtain the effects next described.

Thumb Step III

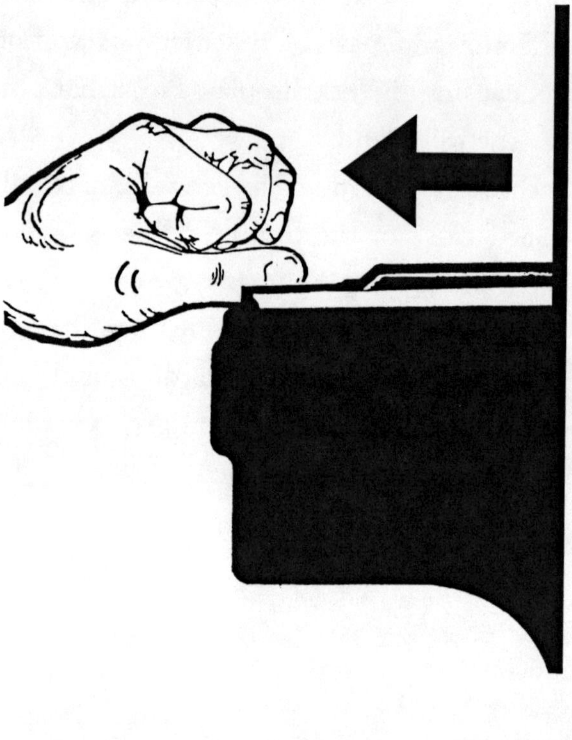

Thumb Step III

Just as Step IV in the previous chapter was the pivotal idea for improving the touch for fingers two through five, Thumb Step III is the pivotal idea which will give the thumb a controlled, beautiful touch. That's because Thumb Step III exercises the internal thenar muscles, which have been overlooked in the past. Thumb Step III, together with Thumb Step IV, provide the thumb with proper balance and control.

The secret for exercising those internal thenar muscles is that you do not move the thumb to achieve this. In fact, a reverse process is needed. You have to leave the thumb immobile and act upon it with the index finger!

However, for the thumbs there is no external check to overdoing their exercises. There is nothing comparable to the black keys, which halt the rotation of the other four fingers. Therefore, let the check for the thumb exercises be internal—follow this thumb step precisely.

Leaving the thumb on the depressed key, slowly retract the hand so that only the last thumb phalanx is on the key. Flex the index finger so that it folds into the palm, right next to the thumb. You will see, as well as feel, the internal thenar contract.

Do not hold the flex in this position, but proceed immediately to Thumb Step IV. In other words, Thumb Steps III and IV will actually constitute one smooth motion.

Thumb Step IV

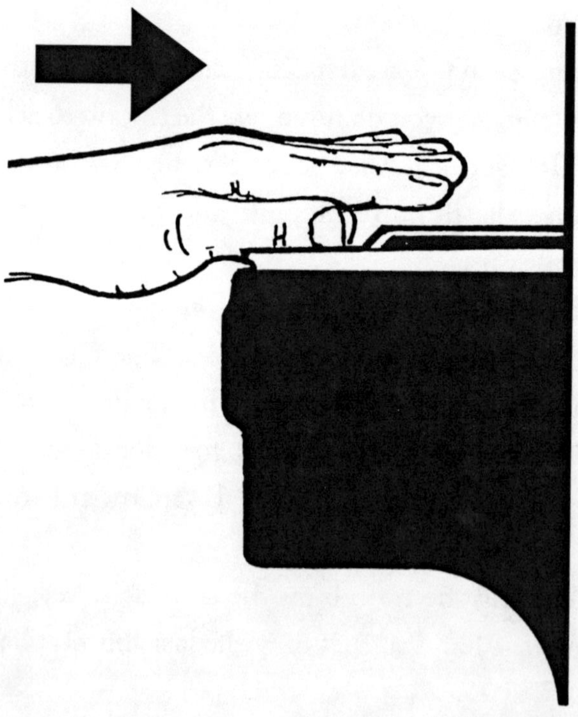

Thumb Step IV

Reverse the process. That is, the instant the index finger touches the palm, immediately extend it fully and slide the hand forward so that both thumb phalanxes rest on the white key, the same position as in Thumb Step II. Hold that position and say the word 'and.'

Thumb Step V

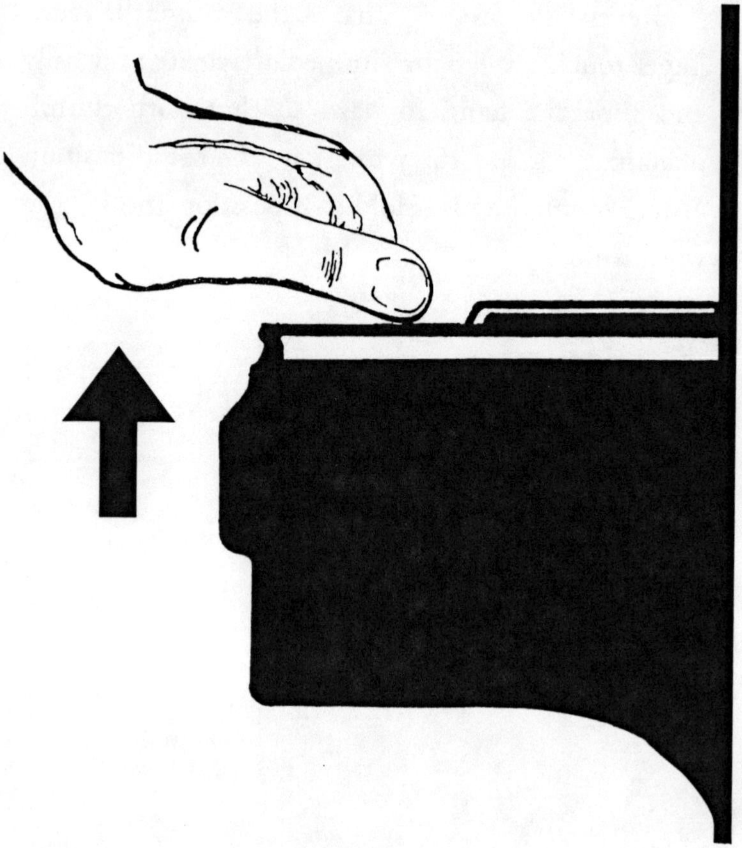

Thumb Step V

Raise the left wrist so that the first thumb phalanx (nearest the hand) lifts off the key at about a fifteen-degree angle to the keyboard. The distal side of the last thumb phalanx will still be depressing the key. Hold that position and say the word 'and.'

Thumb Step VI

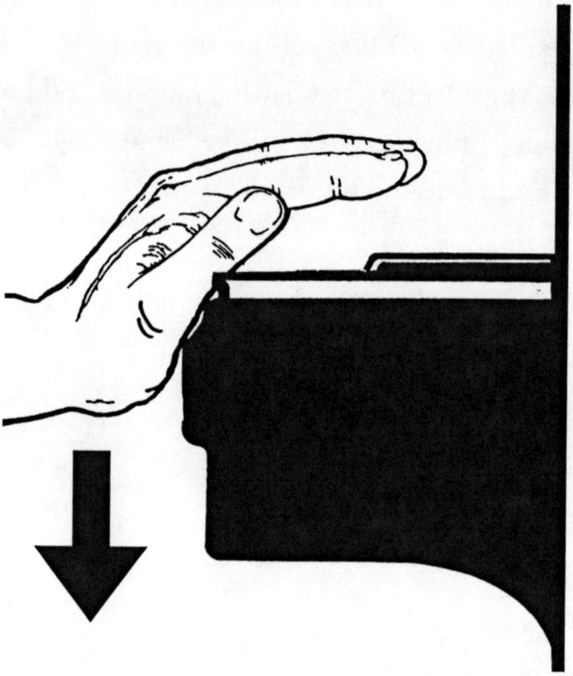

Thumb Step VI

Drop the wrist into low position. This will lift the last thumb phalanx off the key and place the entire hand back into the Thumb Step I position again—left palm against the piano frame at about a 45 degree angle to the keyboard. The first phalanx of the left thumb will rest against the key being practiced. This is the thumb 'drop.' Hold that position and say the word 'and.'

In addition to exercising the extensor muscles in the forearm, dropping the wrist into low position performs the vital function of exercising the external thenar muscles in the hand.

This retraction completes the practicing of a note with the thumb. Repeat this training exercise as often as necessary, using the same or different keys, to warm up the left thumb.

Thumb Step VII

Execute Steps I to VI for the right thumb, using the two octaves above middle C, until the right thumb is warmed up. Then, go back and forth, practicing first one thumb and then the other a few times until you feel both are warmed up.

Because the effects of the thumb exercises are so major, you may choose to exercise the thumbs before the other fingers. Whichever you choose to do first, thumbs or fingers, the results will be the same. Then proceed as the following chapter indicates.

Chapter 5

Adjustments for Practicing Pieces

ONCE YOU HAVE MASTERED the training exercises on the designated white keys, which will take a comparatively short period of time, you will be ready to make the adjustments necessary for practicing (not playing) pieces. As you come to each note, do the exercise for the designated finger.

Note that in Chapter II, the difference between Step III and Steps I and V is slight. That is, in Step III the entire palm touches the piano frame, whereas in Steps I and V only the top of the palm touches the piano frame. When you practice pieces, it makes sense to segue from Step V for one note right into Step II of the next note. That gives the practicing a palpable flow. The loss in flexor contraction is very small and, in any event, will be made up for either in your own adjunct technique or merely from playing the pieces themselves.

In the warm-up, some of the white keys and all of the black keys were omitted. For practicing the previously omitted white keys you will, of course, not have the support of an adjacent black key. Consequently, the finger will not be as anchored, nor the rotation as strong as it had been on the practice keys. However, there is another option if you feel the need for further support: as you supinate the finger on these white keys, you can extend the finger and hand forward until the finger presses against the fall board (the moveable section of the piano which covers and uncovers the keys).

When practicing the black keys (for fingers 2 to 5), depress the black key toward the edge nearest middle C with the last phalanx of the finger. Then supinate the wrist, which will invert the finger playing the black key over the adjacent white key. Then reverse the movements just as you learned it in Chapter II.

When you practice on a black key with the thumb, a few adjustments must be made. First of all, you have to move your hand forward, onto the keys, in order to play a black key with the thumb. There may not be room enough to extend the other four fingers directly toward the fall board. In that case extend those four fingers at a 45 degree angle to the thumb.

Instead of Thumb Steps I and II, depress the black key from that position. Execute Thumb Steps III and IV on the black key. For Thumb Step VI, the 'drop,' all you'll be able to do is let the palm depress the white keys. Then retract the thumb and hand until the thumb is off the black key. The palm will once again be depressing the white keys. Since, presumably, you will next be using another finger besides the thumb, continue to retract the hand until the top of the palm is back against the piano frame, in proper position to practice that other finger.

What about practicing intervals and chords? Since the warm-up and practicing individual notes of pieces give the extensor muscles such a thorough training, I have found that using the 'drop' for intervals and chords (Step III/Thumb Step VI), thereby practicing all the notes simultaneously, suffices the great majority of the time. Usually it is not necessary to utilize rotations.

But in case there is a particularly difficult passage of intervals or chords, I break it down. First I train each finger for each note separately, using rotations, doing the entire exercise for each finger one at a time. Then I practice the full interval or chord, and 'drop' at the end.

For example, in Chopin's Polonaise in A flat, after the initial E flat chords, the right hand has successive augmented thirds. It begins on E and A below middle C, then chromatically ascends until B flat and E flat are played. When I practiced the thirds as intervals I could not get the clarity of hearing separate intervals, let alone the touch I wanted. So I broke it down. First I practiced the E and A separately; then I practiced them as an interval. And so on, for each interval up to B flat and E flat. Then I practiced all the intervals in succession. Then I practiced the left-hand single notes in succession. Finally, I put the whole thing together, forming the successive two-hand chords Chopin wrote with individualized clarity together with the swiftness the passage calls for, and at the same time, with the touch I wanted to evoke the emotions inherent in the music.

With my thumb exercise you will probably have a new sensation when playing intervals and chords. Even though the thumb is being played simultaneously with other fingers, you should experience a feeling of the synchronization of two separate forces at work.

Conclusion

TRADITIONAL EXERCISES do not sufficiently address the important problem of touch. What is neglected, and evidently has not even been conceived of, is the necessity for training the antagonistic extensor muscles. My method trains these muscles. It is specifically designed to achieve the development of extensor muscles, bringing them into balance with the flexor muscles in the hands and forearms, leading directly to a sensitive control of one's touch.

In addition, these exercises may also minimize the risk of injury. The natural, harmonious interaction of muscles delineated in this work should, I think, provide a bulwark against such injuries.

My training program can be used as an adjunct to whatever technique you are currently employing for your practicing. In no way does it interfere with or contradict other practicing methods. Rather it complements them, because it trains muscles other methods omit.

Or my training program can be used alone. I myself have been using only this practicing method for many years. I have achieved what I set out to do. I have acquired a touch which enables me to sound in reality the way I hear music in my mind. My finger articulation is crisper and cleaner than it ever was before. And all with delicious, guiltless freedom from those boring childhood exercises.

I don't mean there isn't work involved. Of course there is. The more I practice, the better I sound, and the closer to that internal ideal I come. Perfect, never. But now I always hear my piano sing.

Whether you use my method alone or as an adjunct to your current practicing program, I believe you will discover how your fingers can create the most beautiful sound your heart is capable of. Truly magical.

Appendix

This appendix is about piano techniques that prior theorists have put forth. I have chosen some representative examples from the various sources used in my research. These examples are from both the scientific and artistic schools of thought. Necessarily I epitomized their works, which most often were extensive and thorough.

Ludvig Deppe

The modern era of piano technique is generally thought to have begun with Ludvig Deppe. Deppe felt that, unlike the voice and the violin, there existed at the time no cohesive approach to playing the piano. He claimed to have accomplished that. Like Bach before him, Deppe felt that the seat at the piano should be low—in fact he attributed frequently recurring arm strain to too high a seat. However, it should only be low enough to enable the pianist to have his/her forearm slightly raised. Tone production, for Deppe, was developed through the weight of the hand. The low seat allowed for a more erect, relaxed posture, which would reduce nervous tension as well.

A pupil of Deppe's lamented to her landlady that she hadn't met him four years previously. Meanwhile her studies had been unsuccessful. The landlady's advice to her tenant is worthy of note. The pupil should rejoice at having met Deppe at all; so many people go through life without ever meeting the right teacher.

Deppe also emphasized the proper functioning of the upper arm and shoulder muscles, even proposing exercises for this—which was something earlier theorists were hardly aware of. Deppe recommended exercises away from the keyboard, such as the use of horizontal bars.

In fact, gymnastics has been recommended since the early 19th century. For example, Ridley Prentice (1842-1895) stated that the same set of muscles was always exercised during practicing. Other arm muscles were ignored. Therefore players' muscles were out of balance (Editor's note: These exact conditions are what my practice exercises correct).

Thomas Matthay

Matthay was known for his concept of forearm rotation. He posited two kinds of rotation—visible and invisible. By visible he meant the obvious physical movements. By invisible he meant rotary stresses and reactions, mostly unaccompanied by any movements whatsoever. He himself stressed the invisible type of rotation. Human nature being what it is, people often misunderstood him and continued stressing the visible rotary movements.

Matthay's aim was to have all the fingers, including the pinky and the thumb, apply equal weight to the keys. Since it is clear, for example, that the thumb is inherently much stronger than the pinky, that equality should be achieved, or at least approached, through these invisible rotatory actions or stresses. Matthay formulated exercises to facilitate making these rotations. (Editor's note: thus Matthay's exercises, and all the time and effort involved in doing them, were conceived as the cause of, and therefore the necessary precursors to, the rotations; for the present author, such rotations would be the natural result of doing his exercises—without the burden of conscious thought or practice).

Otto Ortmann

Ortmann was also concerned with visible and invisible characteristics. His orientation stressed physiological aspects such as muscular exertion and coordination, weight application, relaxation, and the importance of the circulatory system's blood supply to the fingers and that blood supply's effect on technical proficiency—for which he recommended warm-up time at the keyboard, not only for recitals, but even for lessons.

Ortmann also was very concerned with the physical aspects of the piano instrument. He contradicted theories that percussive touches caused hammers to quiver, showing that the only factor responsible for string vibration was the velocity of the hammer. Therefore, he concluded, essential differences in tone quality were primarily derived from differences in hammer speed. Scientific measurements have supported this claim, demonstrating that the speed of the last eighth of an inch the hammer travels before striking the strings varies between 416 hundred thousandths of a second to produce the softest pianissimo note and 51 hundred thousandths to produce the loudest forte note.

What was left unsolved is the question of how the pianist could control his/her touch so as to produce speeds between the 51 hundred thousandths of a second and the 416 hundred thousandths of a second at will. Not that one should know the exact number of hundred thousandth seconds each hammer uses, of course, but that one's touch should be so honed as to be able to feel and produce minute changes in volume with a high degree of accuracy, thereby being able to produce a wide range of tones. In other words, Ortmann's work, as laudable as it was, did not solve the problem of how to produce a singing tone on the piano when one wanted to, nor to vary legato and percussive tones at will. He certainly recognized that the relation and variety of consecutive individual tones are what will achieve a beautiful tone on the piano. He also held, rightly in my view, that it is imperative to be able to have a high degree of control over the touch for each individual tone before one considers the flow and sound quality of consecutive tones. However, he did not translate those ideas into a cogent technique.

Arnold Schultz

Schultz wrote about finger coordination, stressing that each finger phalanx should be considered individually. Schultz considered the thumb as having the least complex coordination to analyze, possibly because the thumb action is confined to the first phalanx in its joint near the wrist.

Schultz considered it axiomatic that a study of finger coordination necessarily had to be based upon an understanding of the finger's musculature. This is a very good idea, as far as it goes. However, he limited that analysis to the muscular coordination of the downward movement of the thumb onto the keys. Schultz failed to see that analysis should go further and include analysis of the musculature when the thumb is raised off the keys.

The following is a more detailed description of Schultz's analysis of thumb musculature. Schultz claimed that five sets of muscles were involved in finger action: (1) the flexor profundis, whose origin is in the under side of the forearm and insertion is into the third phalanx (the finger segment to which the fingernail is attached); (2) the flexor sublimis, whose origin is also in the underside of the forearm, but whose insertion is into the second (middle) phalanx; (3) the lumbricalis, whose origin is at the base of the palm and whose insertion is into the first phalanx; (4) the interossei, whose origins are at the base of the palm and whose insertions are into the first phalanx, who function essentially for lateral movements; (5) the extensor communis, whose origin is in the upper side of the forearm and whose insertion is in the third phalanx, the nail segment.

(Editor's note: In my book this classification has been subsumed by the external thenar muscles—Schultz never even considered the internal thenars, the muscles located between the thumb and index finger, as relevant to thumb movement, an oversight regarded herein as a major error).

Schultz called the flexor profundis and the flexor sublimis the long flexors, and the lumbricalis and interossei the small finger muscles. He postulated that if the long flexors and the extensor communis were only used, the fingers would be stiffened, locking all the phalanxes into a unit.

While this would easily produce volume, it would not produce a fine tone.

To achieve the latter, the small muscles would have to be coordinated with the long flexors. This would often call for a flat finger position, which might resemble the stiff finger position he abjured. He regarded that as further testimony for Matthay's position that muscular coordinations are mainly invisible.

Schultz also discussed the use of the small muscles alone. The small muscles pulling only on the first phalanx would propel the fingers downward. There would be a slight extension of the fingers, in addition to their downward movement, because the small muscles have an insertion into the extensor tendon. As the small muscles contract, an opposite action would also occur, namely an upward pull on the second and third phalanxes. This would cause 'broken' mid-joints of the fingers. However, the degree of 'break' could vary. This could happen from a flat finger or curved finger position, so that the intensity of tones would vary as well.

Schultz held that the use of the small muscles with the extensors allowed for the quickest of all finger coordinations. This was because the use of the long flexors involved the displacement of tendons, which necessarily slowed finger coordinations down. Also, since the small muscles only cross the hand-knuckle joints, no tension would be created in the wrist joint, leaving the hand relaxed and free.

To illustrate the sense of freedom which would ensue from only moving the small muscles and the extensor, Schultz suggested that one press a finger into one's thigh without moving any of the joints, then press again but consciously break the mid-joint, then alternate a few times between the two positions. The greater feeling of freedom on the under side of the mid-joint when it is 'broken' should become evident. Schultz went on to describe in detail the sensations one should feel at the mid-joints when employing small muscle coordination.

However, he also went on to describe another finger coordination in which the long flexors would also be included with the small muscles and extensor. Although the inclusion of the long flexors would diminish velocity, if its action and the action of the extensor were minimized this diminished velocity would be minimized as well, while achieving good intensity control.

Schultz then considered the relative functions and merits of various finger positions. A flat finger position, while necessarily expending more energy for increases in intensity, nevertheless has the advantage over a curved or rounded finger position for legato lines. It is particularly adaptive for isolated chords.

Schultz also addressed the problem of wrist level. A high wrist is more efficient to produce force; a low wrist facilitates finger articulation. He felt that, while extremes of both positions were sometimes legitimate, it was generally advisable to maintain a mean position between those extremes.

Schultz came to emphasize relaxation, more and more coming to the position that relaxation was more of a psychological problem, rather than a physiological one. He felt that theorists who addressed relaxation from the physiological viewpoint, however well meaning they may have been, had led the student down the garden path.

Abby Whiteside

A different approach, though not wholly inconsistent with Schultz's later thinking, was made by Abby Whiteside (1881-1956). While she concurred with Ortmann's scientific research, Whiteside asked how he could possibly teach it. In other words, Whiteside was always interested in integrating her theoretical ideas with her pragmatic teaching. She was extraordinarily fluid and flexible in her thinking about how one played the piano keys, continually changing and growing. (Editor's note: Nevertheless, that flexibility was necessarily limited by the parameters of her not having considered the problem of how to get off the keys).

At one point Whiteside stressed the importance of the upper arm. She thought that the pull of the upper arm was the basis of speed without strain and of what she called basic rhythm. Basic rhythm referred to the physical movements, which accompanied musical continuity. Musical continuity meant the flow in the production of a musical phrase, as well as the flow in phrase-to-phrase progressions. Whiteside felt at the time that this basic rhythm was, indeed, the most crucial factor in creating a beautiful performance. In addition, she held that the upper arm was instrumental in gauging the movements for distance on the keyboard. At first blush her claim for the importance of what she called basic rhythm might appear exaggerated. However, this was not just theorizing on her part. She taught this to her students and evidently produced extraordinary improvement in their playing.

However, while Whiteside continued in her firm belief that the upper arm was the prime factor in the coordination of one's playing, during the last twenty-five years of her life she nevertheless altered her view of the manner in which upper arm control was applied many times over. Sometimes her change was modest; sometimes it was drastic. Whiteside was never irrevocably bound to a viewpoint, no matter how long she had held it, when a new idea presented itself and seemed to be an improvement.

Sometime in the early Thirties Whiteside began to explore the idea that the torso governed the pianist's performance. Here her thinking was notable for her ability to completely reverse her approach. Instead of a pull (as she had postulated previously in the upper arms), she felt that the torso acted by means of pushing. Now it was the torso which initiated the basic rhythm. Yet she had not discarded the upper arm pull. Evidently the torso push and upper arm pull existed simultaneously for her.

This phase of her thinking lasted several years, until Whiteside once again reversed ground. She then postulated that the torso's control would be more effective if it initiated the basic rhythm by a pull instead of a push. Once again it was reported that she achieved remarkable results teaching this approach to her students. Whiteside's instincts led her to be concerned with the activity which took place between finger articulations, but her explorations in this regard were confined to bodily rhythms. She even had her students rock and bounce their bodies. Had Whiteside's instincts led her to consider the problem of how one actually got off the keys, who knows, perhaps she might have anticipated the work in this book.

Whiteside continued to develop her torso ideas. For many years she had advocated activating (during practicing) the upper arm as initiator of finding and striking the keys by moving it in an exaggerated arc. The forearms, hands, and fingers, under this rubric, served to transmit the power of the upper arm. Eventually Whiteside changed that so that the torso acted as the power source, with the upper arm now serving as an extension of the torso. She extended this idea to the playing of octaves. The torso would bring the arms down by hunching over, and then lift them by straightening up. Lateral distances on the keyboard would be accomplished simply by a lateral swaying of the torso. Once again, practicing in this way reportedly evinced almost miraculous results for her students.

To her everlasting credit, despite her being convinced of the correctness of her new ideas, Whiteside was prepared to abandon them. The fact was that this new approach did not work for all of her students.

Whiteside had the integrity to admit that if her new technique did not work for some of her students, it could not be completely correct. She did not totally abandon her concept of torso action, but modified it so that she hypothesized that the torso followed the upper arm, rather than leading it.

Ironically, the same critical question Whiteside had about how one would teach Ortmann's scientific findings is pertinent to Whiteside's concepts regarding the functions of the torso and upper arms. I think that this could be accomplished naturally by simply expanding on an idea of Leschetizky. Leschetizky said that the pianist should engage in deep breathing just like the singer. (Editor's note: Modern research defines deep breathing as 'belly' breathing, inhaling by expanding the belly. I contend that belly breathing involves the torso and upper arms without having to think about it. Belly breathing, rather than shallow chest breathing, fosters emotional responsiveness, bodily relaxation, and listening. It engages the entire body in the rhythmic process, and tends to short-circuit any mental impediments. I recommend it highly.)

Whiteside took an antagonistic stance against the exercises of scales and the exercises of Hanon and Czerny, usually so slavishly taught and learned. Her position was that practicing these exercises merely made for facility in playing the exercises themselves. They did not promote one's ability to play the piano well and beautifully. There was no transfer from those exercises to playing, for instance, Bach or Beethoven well.

Hanon's exercises, for example, were aimed at developing equal striking power in each finger. Physiologically, finger inequality exists. Ergo, equal striking power can never really be accomplished. Furthermore, the aim is superfluous, according to Whiteside, since the fingers need only be trained to transmit the power initiated by the upper arm. This is an aim which she thought was both desirable and attainable.

Whiteside maintained that by understanding Nature's way, in this case by comprehending that the upper arm initiates the power for piano playing, and following it, instead of slavishly repeating traditional exercises, pianists would avoid boredom and frustration, and would be utilizing time well instead of wasting it.

Whiteside felt that, during practicing, all the training the pianist needs could be found in Chopin's Etudes. She thought that each Etude brought into focus a different facet of the fundamental pianistic actions, all of which were embraced in toto by the full body of the Etudes.

Whiteside also said that in the playing of chords others had promoted training the fingers to reach for proper key position. She advocated palm control instead. For example, slowly close and open your fist. Note the spreading out of first the palm, then the knuckles, and finally the fingers. Whiteside maintained that only when that kind of palm spreading took place could the wrist remain free and the arm provide the requisite power and control. Incidentally, old motion pictures of jazz greats such as J.P. Johnson, Willie the Lion Smith and Fats Waller, in their piano contests with each other, demonstrated rapid changing chords with the left hand. Those chord changes might be seen as models of what Whiteside meant.

However, Whiteside thought that a separate initiation of power for each tone, a note-by-note procedure, was antithetical to the creation of beautiful piano playing. This was because it seemed obvious to her, as indeed to other theorists (except the present author), that all power for tone production is applied to the keys with a down stroke, and that power had to be applied in a continuous action to produce a beautiful phrase

As far as it goes, that statement is correct. Yes, when we play the keys we are applying power with a down stroke. But when we get off the keys, we are using an up stroke. That up stroke is a subtle preparation for the next down stroke! That up stroke affects both the power and control we apply to that next down stroke. Therefore when we are practicing, a note-by-note procedure that practices each up stroke is absolutely essential to subsequently achieving a flow of beautiful phrasing. In fact, once the individual up strokes are practiced, the phrasing seems to almost flow of its own accord. Practicing the up strokes as taught in this book gives the hands a marvelous sense of freedom, almost as if one's hands had been let out of a cage.

Whiteside's approach to teaching the piano seemed exemplary. It seemed obvious to her that, since playing the piano involved both the physical action of playing the notes and the performer listening to the music s/he is producing, the piano student should begin by playing by ear. Of course students should eventually learn to read music. However, they should be primarily aural learners first. It is only common sense to realize that printed notes are only symbols for sounds, not the sounds themselves. Pupils who learn music by the way it sounds thus hear the sound when they see the symbol. Pupils who learn visually first are forced to go through the mental process of translating the symbols into sounds. Whiteside held that this was not only an unnecessary extra mental process, but that it actually interfered with the natural process of making music. It was Whiteside's opinion that pupils who learned to play by ear played with an ease and accuracy that a sight learner could never quite match.

Whiteside also raised the significant question as to why hosts of people who took piano lessons as children had stopped playing as adults. It was Whiteside's view that the reason lay in the fact that so many had been erroneously taught to be visual learners. Playing the piano, therefore, for them had been a task for keeping in practice, rather than a continuance in delighting to make music.

Whiteside taught that the two basic factors in acquiring musical skill were the feeling of rhythm and the auditory image, which is what the pianist hears in the mind as s/he plays. The very first sensation pupils should experience at the piano is that when they touch the keyboard they bring a melody, however simple, to life. Thus pupils should be emotionally involved with music right from the start. The emotional involvement essential to playing the piano would never result from mere finger exercises. Pupils must begin, according to Whiteside, with the ear, never with the hand. She said that those who begin with the hand are trapped. That way there is a chasm built in the brain between hand mechanics and producing music, a chasm that seldom can be breached, and that perhaps could account for so many adults having given up playing the piano.

Whiteside maintained that there were two rhythms—the rhythm of note-to-note articulation and the rhythm of both phrases and the whole work itself. While the rhythm of the former is essential, it only has meaning if it is subordinate to and fused with the latter. Jazz players as a group are particularly able to meld tunes in their ears with the rhythms involved (Editor's note: just listen to Art Tatum do that). They may embellish melodies, but they keep the rhythm. Whiteside thought that improvisation was a particularly good technique for engaging the ear to listen. In fact she felt that 'keep your ear on the music' should be the musician's motto. She also thought that as a consequence, improvisation would also tend to engage the body in the rhythm. She also advocated a tactic that she named 'splashing.' Splashing is a process of playing the relevant chords in a piece all over the piano without regard either to their accuracy or to the actual melody. Again, Whiteside regarded that as a way of engaging the ear while harnessing the body into rhythmic participation.

Whiteside thought that many professional pianists sounded much better playing concertos than they did in their solo recitals. She thought that the reason for this was that in playing concertos they were compelled to listen and react to the rhythm of the orchestra. The interaction with the orchestra allowed the pianist more emotional involvement in making music. On the other hand, Whiteside thought that in solo recitals too often pianists' minds and hands got between them and the music, rendering their playing disjointed, without meaning.

The ideal way to avoid those pitfalls was, to Whiteside, in the very first piano lessons. It is there, right in the beginning, in pupils' very first piano lessons, where pupils' first and most lasting impressions are formed.

It is imperative, in Whiteside's view, that those impressions should be to feel the over-all rhythm of a piece and hear that piece as an emotional outlet. It should never be a case of struggling to force his/her hands to hit the right keys. I only too well remember my first piano lessons, as well as those of my sister and a host of other children. All of us were taught by a sight-first method which also stressed hand accuracy. The lessons and practice sessions were boring in the extreme. I marvel that my love of music kept me persevering. All of the other children I knew, sooner or later, joined the ranks of ex-pianists. It was really the discoveries described in this book that enabled me to break through to what I heard in my inner ear and through that to engage my body in rhythm. I love the fact that this has accomplished something for my touch which could not have been done any other way. However, there is also the hard truth of what Whiteside said. That initial learning by sight and hand accuracy created damage which I struggle against to this day. I am grateful that I became, in a sense, my own teacher but I want to leave you by urging you not just to use my exercises, but to use them in conjunction with finding a teacher for your children who is, so to speak, in the Whiteside camp, that is one who teaches pupils to first learn by ear.

Bibliography

Anthony, Michael. "The Hazards of Music-making." *New York Daily News.* 5 Oct. 1987: 41.

Bach, Carl Philipp Emanuel. *Essay on the True Art of Playing Keyboard Instruments.* Ed., Trans. William J. Mitchell. New York: W. W. Norton, 1949.

Deppe, Ludwig. *The Deppe Finger Exercises.* Chicago: Musica Obscura,1971.

Fielden, Thomas. *The Science of Pianoforte Technique.* London: Macmillian, 1934.

Freud, Sigmund and Charcot. *Collected Papers* (Vol. I, pp. 9-23). Ed. Ernest Jones. New York: Basic Books, 1959.

Jaell-trautmann, Marie. *Le mecanisme du Toucher; l'etude du piano par L'analyse experimentale de la Sensibilite tactile. (The Mechanism of Touch; the Study of the Piano for Experimental Analysis of Tactile Sensibility).* Paris: A. Colin and Co., 1897.

Jaell-Trautmann, Marie. *La musique et la Psychophysiology*. Paris: F. Alcan, 1926.

Jaell-Trautmann, Marie. *Un nouvel Enseignement artistique; le Toucher musical par l; education de la main. (A New Artistic Education; Musical Touch for the Training of the Hand)*. Paris: Les Presses Universitaires de France, 1927.

Keith, Arthur. "Engines of the Human Body." Paper presented at the Christmas lectures of the Royal Institution of Great Britain, 1916. London: Williams and Norgate, 1920.

Leimer, Karl and Walter Gieseking. *Piano Technique.* New York: Dover Publications, 1972.

Lhevine, Josef. *Basic Principals in Pianoforte Playing.* Forward by Rosina Lhevine. New York: Dover Publications, 1972.

Matthay, Tobias. *The Visible and Invisible in Pianoforte Technique.* London: Oxford University Press, 1932.

Moreno, Jacob. *The Essential Moreno: Writings on Psychodrama, Group Method, and Spontaneity.* New York: Springer Publishing Co., 1987.

Newman, William. *Understanding Music: An Introduction to Music's Elements, Styles, and Forms for Both Layman and the Practitioner.* New York: Harper and Row, 1967.

Ortmann, Otto. *The Physical Basis of Piano Touch and Tone.* London: K. Paul, Trench, Trubner and Co., Ltd., 1925.

Ortmann, Otto. *The physiological mechanics of piano technique.* New York: Dutton, 1929.

Schultz, Arnold. *The Riddle of the Pianist's Finger and Its Relationship to a Touch Scheme.* Chicago: University of Chicago Press, 1936.

Schweitzer, Albert. *Out of My Life and Thought; an Autobiography.* Trans. C.T. Campion. New York: Holt, Rinehart, and Winston, 1949.

Slenczyrska, Ruth. *Music at Your Fingertips.* New York: Doubleday, 1961.

Thrift, Syd, and Barry Shapiro. *The Game According to Syd: the Theories and Teachings of Baseball's Leading Innovator.* New York: Simon and Schuster, 1990.

Tubians, Raoul, *Examination of the Hand and Upper Limb.* Philadelphia: W. B. Saunders Co., 1984.

Whiteside, Abby. *Mastering the Chopin Etudes & Other Essays.* New York: Charles Scribner's Sons, 1969.

Wickiewicz, Thomas. "Muscle Physiology: Implications for Sport Performance." *Sports Neurology.* Ed. D. D. Jordan, P. Tsairis, and R. F. Warren. Baltimore: Aspen Publications, Inc., 1989.

About the Book

Bach and Paderewski, among other keyboard giants, stressed the fact that the thumbs were the most important finger in playing the keyboard. I very much agree that this is a crucial (yet often overlooked) issue in piano technique. The action of the thumbs seriously affects touch on the piano, not only of the thumbs themselves, but of the other fingers as well.

Think of all the things you have done with your hands today: washing, dressing, eating, etc. All of these actions were performed because we possess the remarkable feature of opposable thumbs.

Playing the piano, however, is different, not only from a myriad of life activities, but also from playing other musical instruments. Playing the piano, in fact, is one of the few things in life which require the thumbs not to act in opposition to other fingers, but to act in concert (no pun intended) with them. This unnatural movement causes a problem for the musculature of the thumbs. Obviously you can move your thumbs to depress the keys. But you can't depress the piano keys with the dexterity and sensitivity available to you when you are using the thumbs in their natural, opposable mode. To access that dexterity and sensitivity in the thumbs, to bring the thumb muscles into delicate balance, you must do something to offset the restrictions imposed by the piano.

What is that something? It's an exercise specifically for the thumbs, which I have devised. In my book I explain why a separate thumb exercise is necessary, indeed imperative, to develop a fine touch. Then I show you the exercise, which, although not difficult to do, took me years to conceive of and perfect. When you add this exercise to your practicing, you'll be astounded at the immediate improvement in you touch (and in your practicing generally as well). It will also act as insurance against hand injuries, which are surprisingly more frequent among pianists than one would ordinarily suppose. It's possible that the frequency of hand injuries among pianists is due to the repeated, but subtle, misuse of hand muscles.

Those hand muscles, all of them, should be in delicate balance if a beautiful touch is to be achieved. Thus the book provides a complete picture of exercises for all the other fingers as well, including solving Shumann's famous dilemma about the constriction of the fourth finger, to give your piano a 'singing' sound. You have only to try it to feel the dramatic difference this technique will make in your touch.

About the Author

Larry Greenfield has been involved in several careers. As a teacher for many years he taught Kindergarten and many other levels including Community College. He was written about in Nat Hentoff's book, "Our Children Are Dying."

As a Clinical School Psychologist, Larry again worked with various age groups, from Kindergarten to High School. He invented a technique for employing empathy in the process of interpreting responses to the Rorschach cards. This necessitated formulating a methodology, which can be adapted for solving 'impossible' problems in any field in which one has background.

In retirement from teaching and psychology, Larry is involved with theater groups and has a part-time career doing voice-overs. He is the author of an article, which presents a new approach to creating power in one's voice.

Finally, Larry has always made time to play the piano and to devote to it years of thought and experimentation. That work has culminated in this book. He hopes that you do his exercises. If you try them, he has no doubt at all that you will be astounded by the improvement in the beauty of your playing.

Larry also thinks the exercise in his method will go a long way in preventing injuries, not only to pianists, but also to computer users. All that computer users will need to adapt his method is a flat, horizontal surface. This should definitely alleviate most of the injuries computer users have endured.

Printed in the United States
64971LVS00003B/35